I BELIEVE

A Philosophy for the Global Society

Price : Rs. 125.00 (Rupees One hundred twenty five only)

Edition : 2008
ISBN : 978-81-7028-747-6
I BELIEVE : A Philosophy for the Global Society (Philosophy)
by Dr Karan Singh
(First published in 2006 by Bharatiya Vidya Bhawan, Mumbai)

RAJPAL & SONS, Kashmere Gate, Delhi-110006
e-mail : mail@rajpalpublishing.com
website : www.rajpalpublishing.com

I BELIEVE

A Philosophy for the Global Society

Dr Karan Singh

rajpal

I BELIEVE

A Philosophy for the Global Society

Dr. Karan Singh

To

Asha

my life companion

Akhanada Saubhâgyavati Bhava

PREFACE

As I travel around the world I am often asked, usually by younger people, a simple but formidable question : *"What is your philosophy?"* While I speak extensively on the philosophy of *Vedanta*, of the *Upanishads,* of Sri Aurobindo and so on, that does not answer the question. So I thought I would try and spell out what precisely I believe.

Our beliefs flow from the totality of experience to which we have been exposed. I have been fortunate that my exposure has in many ways been more varied and intense than falls to the lot of most people. There are four main sets of factors that have moulded my thinking – books, music, travel, and people. In all four I have had the good fortune of an extremely wide and stimulating contact, and if I have not imbibed more from them the fault is entirely my own. In any case, I shall try briefly to identify the major beliefs I have come to hold, even though I am acutely aware of the difficulty in expressing complex ideas in simple words :

1. I believe that man, still in an intermediate stage between the animal and the divine, can raise himself to a higher plane of being if he makes a conscious and dedicated effort to do so; and there can be no nobler endeavour than this aspiration towards divinity. I believe that each human being born on this planet, or for that matter anywhere else in the limitless cosmos, carries within themselves an unquenchable spark of divinity. Our true destiny as human beings revolves around fanning of this spark into the smokeless flame of spiritual realization.

2. I believe that all political, economic, and social activities should have as their ultimate goal the fostering of this divinity within each individual. Scientific and technological developments are ultimately counter-productive if they do not lead us towards this end.

3. I believe that at their highest all religions are so many different paths leading to the same goal, the ineffable and indescribable union between the human and the divine; that mystics of all religious persuasions have realized and preached essentially the same doctrine of human love and divine communion; and that strife and hatred in the name of religion is therefore (see p. 33) the very antithesis of spirituality and a gross slur on the name of humanity.

4. I believe that India, with its unique heritage stretching back to the very dawn of civilization, has a special role to play in fostering a society which would support this process of evolution. In a world

torn by violence and hatred I believe that India can play a crucial role in leading humanity towards a new equilibrium between wealth and wisdom, having and being. I believe that we must work for political integration, economic growth, social transformation, and secular democracy not merely as ends in themselves but because this combination can best provide the framework within which the people of our ancient land can fulfill their destiny.

5. I believe that as long as millions go without the basic necessities of civilized existence it is utterly unreal to talk to them about things of the spirit, and that the basic material needs of man must be satisfied as a foundation for further spiritual growth. I believe that this can be achieved only when we succeed in motivating the people of India to put in several decades of hard, disciplined effort for the production of wealth and simultaneously adopt policies to ensure that the wealth so produced is distributed fairly to all sections of society. I believe that this can be achieved not by propagating the bitter doctrine of implacable class warfare but, rather, by trying to involve the nation as a whole in the mighty effort required to break the poverty barrier that still persists around us.

6. I believe that politics will always be turbulent because that is the nature of politics, as it is the nature of the sun to be hot and water to be wet, and that we must face boldly the battle of life into which we find ourselves precipitated. I believe that, approached in

the right spirit, political activity can be a powerful instrument for human transformation and can thus contribute substantially to the broader goals that lie before the human race.

7. I believe that our generation holds the present in trust for posterity, and that we have to fulfil this responsibility so that we can repay the debt we ourselves owe to the past. I believe that we must, therefore, protect this planet from wanton despoliation and blatant exploitation in the name of progress, that we must conserve its atmosphere and water, its forests and wild life, from the destruction they are facing as the result of increasing urbanization and industrialization.

8. I believe that life is necessarily a mosaic of joy and sorrow, of pleasure and pain, of failure and success, of shadow and sunlight; that we must accept these dualities as a necessary stage in our spiritual progress until we are able to transcend them; and that each experience can be a valuable means for inner growth, unpleasant situations often affording greater opportunities for development than superficially pleasant ones.

9. I believe that love and friendship constitute the surest bonds in a world where everything is constantly changing, and that these should be cherished whenever and wherever they are found. I believe that the creation of beauty through music and poetry, the fine arts and architecture, is a central function of civilization and must be encouraged so that

increasingly large sections of society can derive the intangible (as on p. 83) but extremely valuable benefits that flow therefrom, so that man can be led from the outer beauty of form to the inner beauty of spirit. I believe, further, that our system of education should be designed to inculcate in the young an awareness of the primacy of the spirit, without in any way belittling the importance of the material foundations upon which any dynamic civilization must rest.

10. I believe that while each one of us owes a deep debt to the country of our origin, as members of the human race we also owe a wider loyalty to the planet that has nurtured our kind for millions of years.

11. I believe that death is a natural and necessary corollary to life, and must be accepted in a positive manner rather than with fear and dread. I believe that the death of the body merely marks another step in the long journey of the pilgrim soul towards its final destination, and that man must shake off the superstitious dread that he has with regard to this essential and inescapable phenomenon. One of Lord Shiva's appellations is *Mahakaleshwar*, the Great Lord of Death, and when He is ready, so am I.

12. I believe, finally, that a divine destiny pervades the cosmos, a destiny not distant and remote but one in which, in some mysterious way, each one of us is actively involved. I believe that the most effective means of fulfilling that destiny is a combination of active outer involvement in furthering human

welfare and intense inner striving to reach the goal of spiritual realization. I believe, thus, that the most eloquent prayer that has ever been evolved is one that has resounded in India down through the corridors of time since the very dawn of our civilization:

From illusion lead me unto Reality,
From darkness lead me unto Light,
From death lead me unto Immortality.

Humanity today stands at a crucial crossroads in its long and torturous history on this planet. We now have the resources, if used with wisdom and compassion, to ensure for every human being on Planet Earth at least the minimum material and intellectual inputs necessary for a decent human existence. In our own country we still have to overcome a huge backlog of illiteracy, unemployment and deprivation caused by centuries of feudal rule and colonial domination. But apart from the major poverty elimination project, which must be our over-riding concern, there is the eternal question of living life in a harmonious and integrated manner.

The ideas articulated in this book, if taken together, could perhaps help in evolving an integrated philosophy for the troubled age in which we live, a curiously ambiguous age full of unprecedented opportunity along with continued conflict and clash of ideologies, nationalisms, even of civilizations. I have drawn upon numerous thinkers from India and across the world, as well as upon my own experience of over half a century of active involvement in public affairs, and have tried to present my beliefs in as coherent and integrated a manner as possible. Whether or not I have succeeded in doing so, is for the reader to decide.

–Karan Singh

March 9, 2008

1

I believe that man, still in an intermediate stage between the animal and the divine, can raise himself to a higher plane of being if he makes a conscious and dedicated effort to do so; and there can be no nobler endeavour than this aspiration towards divinity. I believe that each human being born on this planet, or for that matter anywhere else in the limitless cosmos, carries within himself an unquenchable spark of divinity. Our true destiny as human beings revolves around the fanning of this spark into the smokeless flame of spiritual realization.

The great evolutionary philosopher Sri Aurobindo has expounded the theory of spiritual evolution in which the next stage in human consciousness will be a quantum leap from the mental to the supramental, a leap even more dramatic than that which took place in the transition from animal to human consciousness. Be that as it may, I believe that there is within each individual a spark of the divine, call it the *Atman*, the soul, the *Bodhichitta* or by whatever name. It is this spark that energizes human consciousness, and although it is heavily smothered under our physical, emotional and mental awareness, it exists there "within the farthest golden sheath" as the *Upanishad* says. This being the case, each human individual has a unique value, because he or she represents a special co-relation of forces revolving around a spiritual core of which they may or may not be conscious. And the whole enterprise of joining this inner spiritual core with the divine that pervades all existence constitutes what is known as *Yoga*.

The word *'yoga'* has of late acquired a rather superficial connotation, having come to mean only some physical and breathing exercises which seek to further our physical and mental well being. This is certainly important, but in its deeper meaning *yoga* – which comes from the same root as the English word 'yoke' – is a much more comprehensive concept. Broadly speaking, we can identify four main paths of *yoga* – the *yoga* of wisdom (*Jnana yoga*), the *yoga* of love (*Bhakti yoga)*, the *yoga* of works (*Karma yoga*) and the *yoga* of psycho-spiritual disciplines (*Raja yoga*).

Jnana yoga, or the way of wisdom, involves an intellectual discrimination between the real and the unreal, seeking to access the reality that lies behind the manifested universe. In the West this would be somewhat like the concept of Plato who, in the famous parable of the cave, said that all we see are shadows of reality thrown on the wall of the cave, while remaining unaware both of the actual figures and the light that shines on them from behind. The *Upanishads* are par excellence the texts of the *Jnana yoga.* We must understand, though, that this *yoga* does not simply imply a sharpening of the intelligence as we know it, but a movement into a new dimension of awareness in which we see the unity behind the diversity of the world around us. This vision of oneness – which the *Upanishad* calls *'Ekatvam'* – transforms the ordinary human being into a seer, one who sees the integral unity behind the multifarious and bewildering multiplicity of our daily existence. Sri Ramana Maharshi is a quintessential symbol of the *Jnana Yogi.*

If the *Jnana yoga* is the way of the refined intellect, the

Bhakti yoga is the way of the heart illuminated by love and adoration for some personalized aspect of the divine. It virtually means falling in love with one's chosen deity, and thereby offering oneself heart and soul to its service. In the Hindu tradition there is a whole galaxy of deities representing various facets of the all-pervasive divinity. Thus one can worship Shiva or Vishnu, Rama or Krishna, Ganesha or Hanuman or, interestingly, feminine manifestations of the divine such as Durga or Kali. In the Western tradition Jesus Christ himself is par excellence the focus of devotion, and there have been great *bhaktas* like St. Francis of Assisi, St. John of the Cross and St. Teresa of Avila. In Islam the most dramatic manifestation of the *Bhakti yoga* lies in the amazing world of the *Sufis.* Men like the great Maulana Jalaluddin Rumi of Persia, Khwaja Moinuddin Chisti of Ajmer, Hazrat Nizamuddin Aulia of Delhi or Sheikh Nooruddin of Kashmir, were representatives of the dynamic force of love and harmony. The dramatic dance of the dervishes in Turkey is one of the most moving and authentic manifestations of the *yoga* of devotion in this day and age.

Hinduism is replete with *bhaktas,* from Lalleshwari in the North, down to the Shaiva and Vaishnava saints – the Nayanmars and the Alwars – in the south; from Narsi Bhagat, Tukaram and Namdev in the west to Mirabai, Surdas, Tulasidas in the Indo-Gangetic plains, on to Sri Chaitanya Mahaprabhu, Sri Ramakrishna and Shri Shankardeva in the East, to mention only a few. The opening of the heart centre is one of the most powerful methodologies for achieving direct contact with the divine.

As we move on to the *Karma yoga* we come to an aspect that is particularly useful in this day and age, and has been famously expounded in the 'Gita'. Act we must, whether it is the subconscious activities within our bodies, or the conscious acts that we perform in our daily lives. Without such action human civilisation itself would never have developed. But the major question is as to how these actions can be reconciled with the spiritual quest. It is this conundrum that has been addressed by the concept of *Karma yoga* whereby every action that we undertake, whether a great decision that affects the destiny of millions or a small personal act of kindness and compassion, must be dedicated to one's chosen divinity. Thus every act itself becomes worship. Rather than being obsessed with the results we must act from what we consider to be highest level of our consciousness, inwardly dedicate that act to the divine and leave the results to unfold as they may. This is what Mahatma Gandhi meant when he stressed the importance of adopting right means to achieve right ends, for in some ways the means are more important because those are within our control, whereas the ends lie in the womb of the future.

It is important to stress that not every action can be considered *Karma yoga*. Actions flowing from hatred and fanaticism, cruelty and exploitation, can never be considered *Karma yoga* because by definition they are incapable of being offered to the divine. Again good deeds by themselves, while certainly preferable, do not constitute *Karma yoga* unless there is a clear and unequivocal dedication to one's chosen deity. Given such dedication, a process of *Karma yoga* can gradually refine our consciousness and bring us closer to our spiritual goal. Swami Vivekananda and Mother Teresa were two powerful practitioners of *Karma yoga* and left an indelible impress on the world.

The fourth dimension of *yoga* in this brief review is called *Raja yoga,* the royal path which involves psycho-spiritual practices including the physical and breathing exercises that are known as *yoga* around the world. It is important to remember that while these exercises certainly help to develop our physical and mental powers, they would qualify as *yoga* only if they are directed ultimately beyond them to the quickening of the spiritual consciousness. There is a vast corpus of fascinating literature on this subject, but it will suffice to say that the basic theory revolves around the existence of a self-conscious spiritual power that is located at the base of the spine. Under certain circumstances, which include fairly severe discipline and prolonged practice, this power can start to move up the spine, energizing, as it rises, seven *chakras* or plexuses, which bring about incremental transmutation of consciousness, until finally the blazing light of this power – known as *Kundalini,* the serpent power – pours into the cortex thus completing the process of spiritual transmutation. In the West Christian, Jewish and Islamic saints have borne testimony to such awakenings which are often accompanied by super-normal powers.

To conclude, it is important to remember that these four *yogas* are not necessarily mutually exclusive. It is possible, and indeed desirable, that in the very difficult times in which we now live we should utilise as many of these paths as possible so as to fulfil our true destiny as human beings which revolves around the fanning of the divine spark within us into the smokeless flame of spiritual realisation.

2

I believe that all political, economic, and social activities should have as their ultimate goal the fostering of this divinity within each individual. Scientific and technological developments are ultimately counter-productive if they do not lead us towards this end.

Prima facie it is self-evident that political, economic and social activities should have, as their goal, the furthering of the welfare of various sections of society. However, if we are overtaken by a tsunami of hyper-consumerism and ultra-promiscuity, if our television and movies are full of horror and violence, along with a curious obsession with death, disaster and dinosaurs, if the world economic order functions in a manner that increases the gulf between the rich and the poor so that today at least one-third of the world's population—two billion human beings—live below poverty line and another two billion are barely able to manage a decent existence, then all the progress that we have made in so many different fields becomes counter-productive. Social tensions are steadily increasing; the population explosion continues unabated and is already causing a massive problem of illegal migrants, refugees and a shameful trafficking in human beings.

It is necessary, therefore, that our political, economic

and social activities should be endowed with a wider sense of purpose and social commitment. Politically the nation state remains a predominant institution despite its erosion from within by sub-national movements and its transcendence by regional groupings such as the historic and unique European Union. In my view, the nation state must continue to play a central role in providing good governance, though many of its activities may inevitably in due course be subsumed within larger political groupings. The fascinating experiment of the European Union needs to be replicated in other parts of the world. Brought up as we were reading European history replete with unending conflicts for centuries between the European powers on the continent and in their respective colonies, it is quite astounding to see how the European Union has enabled France, Germany and Great Britain, for example, to overcome their age-old hostility and move towards a close economic and political collaboration.

In the last century millions died on the battlefields of Europe in the First and Second World Wars, but today it is possible to travel without a passport from Norway to Greece and from Portugal to Poland. Territorial conflicts such as Alsace-Lorraine and Trieste have virtually disappeared from the European consciousness. It is true that nationalisms continue to be influential, as the recent rejection by some major European poweres of the proposed European Constitution has shown. Nonetheless, the fact that all the currencies of Europe with the exception of Switzerland and the United Kingdom have now disappeared and have been subsumed in the Euro is in itself a most remarkable achievement. In my view, the regional groupings such as the European Union, the ASEAN and our own SAARC represent a necessary stage in the evolution of a truly global community. Indeed a 'final settlement' on Jammu & Kashmir could also be envisaged in this broader regional context.

The United Nations set up over 60 years ago, as successor to the League of Nations, has unfortunately become ineffective and unrepresentative of the emerging global consciousness. The fact that the five major victors of the Second World War continue to appropriate to themselves the exclusive right of Veto and permanent membership of the Security Council detracts from the democratic ideal of the United Nations. While it is true that a one-vote one-nation situation whereby Nauru and Vanuatu have an equal vote with India and China is also irrational, appropriate regional groupings would help to bring about a more coherent and rational global confederation. This attempt to democratize and rationalize the United Nations must necessarily be one of our major pre-occupations in the years and decades ahead.

Science and technology have indeed wrought wonders and marvels far beyond anything that could have been imagined even half a century ago. The breaking of the space barrier by Yuri Gagarin in 1961 and the landing on the moon of Neil Armstrong in 1969, together mark a critical turning point in human history. For the first time a creature of Earth was able to break the gravity barrier that has enclosed us like some invisible iron eggshell ever since we began our long and tortuous evolution on this planet. The subsequent intensive exploration and probes of the solar system have brought back the most amazing photographs of the cosmos whose dimensions far exceed anything that has ever been imagined. The closest description I can think of is the phrase in the *Upanishad* which talks of *"Anantakoti Brahmanda"*, infinite millions of galaxies. Space exploration has always fascinated me, as well as space films such as 'A Space Odyssey 2001' based on a story written by my good friend, the greatest science fiction writer of our times, Sir Arthur Clarke. But here again space exploration can be used both for benign and malign purposes. The attempts to militarise space in order to boost the strategic ambitions of one particular nation are fraught with danger.

This again is a classic dilemma with science and technology. It can do and has done so much to further the welfare of the human race in the field of medicine; for example, the invention of the polio vaccine by another friend the great scientist, Jonas Salk, has saved millions of children from being condemned to a crippled existence and has brought us near the point of polio eradication. Smallpox was eradicated way back in the sixties when I happened to be Health Minister. The new scourge of the HIV/AIDs pandemic is wreaking horrific damage around the world, particularly in the developing countries and especially in sub-Saharan Africa. However, even here biochemists are working on a vaccine as well as a low cost cure. In numerous other fields such as surgery, organ transplant, microbiology, neuro-pharmacology, and also the green revolution, the benign impact of science and technology is clearly visible.

As against this we have seen how science and technology in our own lifetimes have been used for the construction of unimaginable weapons of mass destruction. A single nuclear warhead today packs explosive power equal to a thousand of the bombs that obliterated Hiroshima and Nagasaki in 1945, and it is estimated that as many as 30,000 such nuclear warheads exist today on planet Earth. To take an earlier example, Hitler's gas chambers represented the use of technology for the most horrific and ghastly of all purposes, the mass extermination of millions of human beings just because they belonged to a certain religion.

Two more examples can be given of the hubris that often accompanies technological achievements. The first is the fabled city of Atlantis, which we come across in the writings of Plato. It was a civilization glittering with all the marvels of technology, unrivalled at that time in the world. And one night, we are told, it sank below the waves, unable to survive its own technological ingenuity. A more recent example was the great ship the "Titanic", which was supposed to be unsinkable, equipped as it was with all the latest that technology could provide. On its inaugural voyage the cream of the glitterati and aristocracy of Europe boarded it amidst great festivities and it set sail for the United States secure in the belief that technology had made it invulnerable. It was unaware, however, of the icebergs that were looming up ahead in the dark, and on the very first night it struck against them and sank to the bottom of the sea taking hundreds of passengers with it. Unless technology is tempered with wisdom, it can often become a force for destruction rather than progress. The lesson that we must learn from all this is that simply worshipping science as if it was an undiluted good in itself is unacceptable unless accompanied by compassion, and that the very science that has given us so much progress can, if misused, destroy not only the human race but all life on planet Earth. With the exponential computerization that we are witnessing there is a real danger that the science-fiction notion of electronic machines taking over the planet is not as far fetched as it may once have seemed.

Thus science and technology, if used with wisdom and compassion, can become a major factor in building a sane and harmonious global society in which each human being, on this planet, is assured of at least the minimum physical, material and intellectual inputs for a decent civilised evidence. This must be the ultimate goal of all those in whose hands destiny has placed the control of human affairs.

3

I believe that at their highest all religions are so many different paths leading to the same goal, the ineffable and indescribable union between the human and the divine; that mystics of all religious persuasions have realized and preached essentially the same doctrine of human love and divine communion; and that strife and hatred in the name of religion is therefore the very antithesis of spirituality and a gross slur on the name of humanity.

Religion in history has had a very ambivalent record. On the one hand, much that is great and noble in human civilization—art and architecture, music and dance, literature and moral codes, spiritual classics and gnostic practices—can be traced back to one or other of the great religions of the world. On the other, there has been a long and blood-soaked history of inter-religious and intra-religious conflicts in which millions have perished of inhuman tortures and burnings, widespread persecution and cruelty. So double-edged has the importance of religion been that in many parts of the world large numbers of people have turned away from religion itself. It is here that the Interfaith dialogue assumes critical importance in this era of globalization, because the continuance of religious strife at a time when the technology of destruction has greatly increased represents a grave danger to the human race.

The Interfaith movement, as we now know it, can be

said to have begun in 1893 when the first Parliament of the World's Religions was held in Chicago. It was at this gathering that Swami Vivekananda made an unexpected and dramatic impact with his powerful advocacy of *Vedanta* based upon one of its central teachings—*Ekam sad viprâh bahudhâ vadanti*—the truth is one, the wise call it by many names. Indeed this acceptance of multiple paths to the divine has to be the foundation upon which the whole structure of the Interfaith movement can be built. In the 20th century several significant Interfaith organizations came into being and are still functioning actively, including the Temple of Understanding of which I happen to be Chairman worldwide.

In the course of the last century a large number of Interfaith gatherings were held around the world. The second Parliament of the World's Religions was organized again in Chicago, a century after the first one, in 1993; the third in Cape Town (South Africa) in 1999; and the fourth in Barcelona (Spain) in 2004. These gatherings have brought together thousands of delegates from around the world representing all the main religious traditions and their major sects and denominations. While this impact has been positive, it must be admitted that the Interfaith movement is still peripheral to human consciousness. It is our effort and hope that in the same way as environmental issues moved in the last half century from the periphery to the centre of human concerns, the same will happen to the Interfaith movement in the years ahead.

It is significant here to remark on the extraordinary resilience of religion. I can give two examples—the Soviet

Union was governed by a Marxist-Leninist regime which was firmly committed to atheism. I happened to visit Moscow in 1959 as a guest of Mr. N.S. Khrushchev, the all-powerful General Secretary of the Communist Party of the Soviet Union (CPSU). At a small dinner that he gave for us in the Kremlin I asked him whether it was possible in the Soviet Union to be a member of the CPSU and also a religious believer. He answered categorically in the negative, saying that while they respected religious beliefs, membership of the CPSU necessarily entailed a commitment to atheism. We thus had a regime that ruled the Soviet Union for 70 years during which several generations were indoctrinated against religion. However, as soon as that regime collapsed there was an unprecedented upsurge of religious fervour. I visited Moscow again in 1989 when they were celebrating the one thousandth anniversary of the advent of Christianity, and I was astonished to see the tremendous enthusiasm of devotion, the churches being repaired, the icons repainted and people celebrating the return of religion.

Another example is in Mongolia where the Communist regime mercilessly persecuted the Buddhist monks, destroyed their temples and burnt their scriptures. When that regime collapsed, there was an upsurge of interest in Buddhism, and the people desired once again to recover their lost texts and rebuild their monasteries. It so happened that our Ambassador to Mongolia at that time was the venerable Kushak Bakula, Head Lama of Ladakh. It was he who single handedly was responsible for the re-establishment of Buddhism in Mongolia. He brought back the scriptures and set up a School of Buddhist Studies which I inaugurated during a visit there. Kushak Bakula was greatly revered in Mongolia for doing what Padma Sambhava had done centuries earlier in Tibet. These two examples which I have personally witnessed are enough to show how deeply religion is embedded within the human psyche. It has survived both the Marxist attack and the Fabian neglect.

However all of this raises a serious problem. Today we find that religious fundamentalism has raised its head around the world, particularly the genre lavishly funded by petro-dollars over the last three decades. This is creating havoc in many countries and India is also bearing the brunt of Islamic terrorism and the reactive fundamentalism even in the normally tolerant Hindu society. While appreciating religion, we are faced with the difficult but necessary task of articulating the universal elements in all the great religions of the world rather than the theological fundamentalisms. My experience is that if we concentrate on issues rather than theology, it is easier for harmony to be achieved.

In 1986 a unique gathering was held in Cathedral of St. Francis in Assisi (Italy) where representatives from five great religious traditions—Hindusim, Buddhism, Christianity, Islam and Judaism—were invited to participate in an intensive seminar on 'Man and Nature'. The five delegates were requested to prepare statements on Man and Nature on behalf of their respective traditions, and I had the privilege of writing the Hindu Declaration. These have been subsequently published along with Declarations from three other religions—Jainism, Sikhism and Zoroastrianism, and are known as the Assisi Declaration. It is quite remarkable to see how, despite major and often unbridgeable theological differences, the approach to the question reveals a great deal in common. Similar gatherings directed towards peace, poverty alleviation, HIV/AIDs prevention, the status of women, the environment and so on, can lead to a mutually creative dialogue between religious traditions. Interfaith prayers are also a valuable mechanism for furthering harmony, because when people of different religions pray together it becomes self-evident that in the final analysis, if a divinity does exist, it is not going to be divided into as many religions as are represented. The Interfaith movement is an area in which thinking people around the world must take a deeper interest and show a more effective involvement. Otherwise we are getting into a situation so pithily described by Yeats where

> "the best lack all conviction
> while the worst are full of a passionate intensity"

It is in particular the mystics of all religious persuasions that represent as it were the golden thread of unity cutting across denominational and theological barrier. Whether it is the seers of the Upanishads, the great Jain and Buddhist teachers, the Jewish and Christian mystics, the Islamic Sufis led by Maulana Jalaluddin Rumi or the Sikh *Gurus*, one finds that they have all preached essentially the same doctrine of human love and divine communion. It is these saints who are truly "the salt of the earth", and it is their message of love and harmony that the world needs today as it moves into a global society astride the irreversible arrow of Time.

4

I believe that India, with its unique heritage stretching back to the very dawn of civilization, has a special role to play in fostering a society which would support this process of evolution. In a world torn by violence and hatred I believe that India can play a crucial role in leading humanity towards a new equilibrium between wealth and wisdom, having and being. I believe that we must work for political integration, economic growth, social transformation, and secular democracy not merely as ends in themselves but because this combination can best provide the framework within which the people of our ancient land can fulfil their destiny.

Indian civilization is unique in that, along with the Chinese, it is one of the two longest lasting civilizations in world history. There have been many other great civilizations that flourished in various parts of the world, notably the pharaonic in Egypt, as well as the Mesopotamian and Central and South American civilizations, but they have all passed into history. We can visit the pyramids and gaze at the Sphinx but we cannot contact that vanished civilization. On the other hand, India has an unbroken history at least from *Vedic* times down to the present day. The Indus Valley civilization with its planned cities of Mohanjodaro and Harappa was also an important factor at one point in time, but their disappearance and the decipherment of their script remains one of the few unsolved archaeological mysteries.

The '*Vedas*' constitute the largest corpus of ancient literature available in any of the world's civilizations. In thousands of verses written in the beautiful and evocative

Sanskrit language, hymn after hymn is devoted to almost all aspects of human life, including the famous 'Rg Vedic' Hymn of Creation and the 63 verse Hymn to the Earth in the 'Atharva Veda' which contains surely the most comprehensive ecological statement available in any religious text. It is from the 'Vedic' civilization, with significant developments and inputs from a number of different sources, that the religions known today as Hinduism emerged.

The word 'Hinduism' itself is, of course, a geographical term based upon the Sanskrit name for great river known as the *Sindhu* meaning the flowing one, that lies across the northern boundaries of India. For those living to the east of the river *Sindhu*, which the Greeks called the Indus, came to be known as the land of the Hindus, and the vast spectrum of faiths that flourished here acquired the collective name of Hinduism.

India has in fact been the home of four of the world's great religions, collectively known as the Indic religions. In addition to Hinduism, there were the two great reformist movements of Jainism whose 24th *Tirthankara.* Lord Mahavira was a contemporary of Gautam Buddha who founded Buddhism. Buddhism, of course, although it had a profound influence upon Hindusim, flourished beyond the boundaries of India and reached many countries of South and Southeast Asia all the way down to Japan. The fourth great religion born in India was Sikhism founded by Guru Nanakdev and articulated most forcefully by the Tenth Guru Gobind Singh. In addition to these, several religions came to India from West Asia including the religion of Zarathustra, Prophet of Iran, brought here by the Parsis when they fled from their motherland and sought refuge in India; Judaism, which represents a small but significant element in South India; Christianity which reached India with Saint Thomas in A.D. 57, soon after the passing away of Jesus Christ; and of course, Islam with which Hinduism has had an often troubled relationship over a thousand years.

Each of these religions has added a special flavour to the composite, pluralistic culture of India. Although the Muslims often came here as conquerors and iconoclasts, they also came as traders and, more importantly, brought with them the Sufi saints who preached the message of love and brotherhood and whose shrines—such as those of Khwaja Moinuddin Chisti in Ajmer, Hazrat Nizamuddin Aulia in Delhi and Sheikh Nooruddin Noorani in Chrar-e-Sharif are still venerated by vast numbers of people regardless of their religious persuasions. In Kashmir a unique synthesis was developed between the followers of Kashmir Shaivism whose greatest teacher was Acharya Abhinavagupta and whose last great representative was the woman saint, Lalleshwari, and the Muslim Sufis led by Sheikh Nuruddin. This resulted in what came to be known as the *Rishi* cult which provided a unique spiritual and religious synthesis in the Kashmir Valley.

Despite conquests and massacres, wars and revolutions, India has emerged over the centuries as a confluence of civilizations. It is in this context that I feel India has a special role to play in world affairs. While we are certainly making substantial economic progress, the fact is that our polity has over the last two decades considerably fractured and fragmented, as a result of which hung paraliaments and assemblies are now becoming very much a permanent feature in our political landscape. While coalition governments are an entirely legitimate institution, the large number of political parties involved in the process introduce an element of instability and uncertainty into our political decision making. For India to really rise to its full stature, a strong and coherent government at the Centre is a pre-requisite, while a minority government dependent upon support from outside, howsoever good the leadership, suffers from an inevitable infirmity. The political process in India is still evolving and one must hope that after another one or two General Elections, the position will once again stabilize.

Meanwhile, we must work on three fronts—political integration, economic growth and social transformation in a secular and pluralistic democratic system. It is only if all these factors are tackled effectively that we will be able to overcome the poverty, deprivation and unemployment that we have carried with us into the 21st century. We still have the largest number of illiterates in the world, and more people living below the poeverty line than any other country. This is totally unacceptable and poverty alleviation by 2020 has to be our prime goal.

Meanwhile, India must continue to pull its weight in the international community. It has already become a major regional power and is growing steadily into a country to be reckoned with on the world stage. Our quest for a permanent seat in the U.N. Security Council is eminently justified, although our insistence on the Veto seems to be unrealistic in view of the obvious reluctance of the so-called big five to share their privilege. Indeed the United Nations itself has become, over the decades, an undemocratic and somewhat moribund organization reflecting the post World War II situation rather than contemporary realities. India must continue to press for its due place in the comity of nations, but we must also develop the SAARC as a major regional organization, strengthen our relationship with the ASEAN and Japan. The recent tripartite axis that has been mooted between India, China and Russia represents a most hopeful feature in the creation of a truly multi-polar world.

While Jawaharlal Nehru's policies of *Panchsheel* and non-alignment have obviously outlived their original significance due to dramatic changes in the world situation, the essential idea of developing countries maintaining close and friendly contacts remains valid. It is also necessary for us to strengthen our relationship with the lone super-power in today's world, the United States of America. My contacts with that country go back over half a century when I spent over a year in a New York hospital as a boy, but my brief stint as Ambassador to the U.S. gave me a deeper insight into the manner in which this astonishing country functions. The overriding impression is that within the United States there are multiple centres of power and authority—the White House, the Congress, the Pentagon, the Think Tanks, and, of course, the business and commercial giants. Each one of these plays its role in creating the political equilibrium within the U.S. at any given point in time, and each has the power to influence political decisions so that each needs to be accessed independently if we are to impact the American collective thought process.

A comparatively new and very positive feature is the growing clout of the Indian American community which now numbers well over two million. Our compatriots have done remarkably well in almost every field of public life, whether it is science and technology, medicine and academics, business and commerce. Of late the community has begun to directly impact the electoral process also, particularly at the congressional level, and this is bound to grow in the years ahead. The Indian American community thus represents a major factor for strengthening Indo-American relations. Also the interest of Americans in certain aspects of Indian culture such as *yoga*, ethnic food and dress, dance and music and films represents a significant input. A large number of beautiful Hindu temples built in the United States stand as a testament to the pluralistic culture of that great country, despite the growth of right wing evangelicalism that has been witnessed in recent years.

It needs, however, to be reiterated that in the final analysis the Indian impact on the world will depend upon the level of our own political, economic and social viability. If we can really get our act together, the years and decades ahead could well see India emerging as a truly great power, not merely in military terms but in the broader context of the emerging multi-polar global civilization. This is where the role of the Indian Council for Cultural Relations set up by Maulana Azad soon after independence assumes special significance.

5

I believe that as long as millions go without the basic necessities of civilized existence it is utterly unreal to talk to them about things of the spirit, and that the basic material needs of man must be satisfied as a foundation for further spiritual growth. I believe that this can be achieved only when we succeed in motivating the people of India to put in several decades of hard, disciplined effort for the production of wealth and simultaneously adopt policies to ensure that the wealth so produced is distributed farily to all sections of society. I believe that this can be achieved not by propagating the bitter doctrine of implacable class warfare but, rather, by trying to involve the nation as a whole in the mighty effort required to break the poverty barrier that still persists around us.

Swami Vivekananda once said that to preach religion to a starving person was to insult him; first feed him properly and then give him your religion. Quite clearly, unless we are able to provide to each one of our citizens the minimum inputs necessary for a decent, civilized existence, we have in effect failed as a nation. These minimum inputs include, first of all, necessary nutritional inputs to expectant and nursing mothers and to children at least up to the age of five. It is a tragedy that millions of children in our country are being born stunted in body and mind because they have not received these inputs. What greater deprivation can there be than this, which makes all our talk of our being a great nation sound like empty rhetoric. I recall some decades ago when I was Union Health Minister, there was a programme called the Integrated Child Development Programme (ICDP) which was supposed to have grown to cover our entire population. The fact that it has not done so shows that we have not given adequate priority to these nutritional inputs. The mid-day meal programme is an excellent idea because it ensures all school going children at least one nutritious meal a day, but of course not all of our children go to school.

This brings me to the second input which is education. Our Constitution over half a century ago directed us to provide free and compulsory education to all children up to the age of 14, but we have singularly failed to achieve this, as a result of which there is still a vast army of non-school going children that add to our illiteracy in the country. Unless we give top priority to health and education over the next fifteen years, we will never be able to make up the backlog which is growing steadily as a result of our population growth. Indeed it is a tragic statistic that even though percentage-wise our illiteracy has fallen, in actual numbers we have more illiterate people in India today than we had when we became independent almost six decades ago.

The third input is the provision of at least minimal health services to our entire population. This was to have been achieved through the development of Primary Health Centres and satellite dispensaries in such a way that the whole population is covered. In fact this has not happened and there are still millions of our citizens who are deprived of even rudimentary health facilities. The whole concept of barefoot doctors, village level health workers, and mobile health clinics seems to have got diluted. These three inputs themselves involve a substantial increase in spending on health and education. We had made an international commitment to raise our spending on education to 6 per cent of our GDP, and if 4 per cent is spent on health and family planning then only will we be able to make a substantial dent in this massive challenge by 2020. Obviously this will mean a reordering of our plan priorities, a cutting back of spending in those areas which can be met by the private sector and concentrating upon health and education over the next few years.

Further priorities include dwellings, particularly the massive programme of low-cost housing in the satellite towns. The growth of slums in India has been one of the most negative features in our developmental process. These unplanned cities surrounded by growing slums are like great cancers eating into the heart of the country. Meeting this challenge, of course, involves a broad spectrum of interlocking policies for infrastructural growth and rural development into the details of which it is not possible to go here, but the point needs to be made clearly and unequivocally.

Underlying all of these problems is a factor that unfortunately since the mid-seventies seems to have become radioactive so that no political party is prepared to tackle it head-on. I refer, of course, to the growth in our population. There was at one stage a Marxist theory that population growth was a positive factor because it increases our manpower resources. However, China has proved quite the contrary, and in fact they have gone to the extent of instituting a one-child norm, whereas we seem to have lost all interest in family planning and population control. I do not want to go into details in this regard except to point out that I had presented to Parliament the first National Population Policy way back in 1975 which was a comprehensive statement of political, social and contraceptive measures that were needed. Had my policy continued without a break, we would have substantially lowered the birthrate as well as our total population. Unfortunately, due to factors beyond my control during and after the emrgency, the whole programme got derailed and discredited.

Although some weak attempts have been made recently to recover the lost momentum, I am afraid we have fallen far behind and will now be obliged to face a massive population increase over the next few decades. As it is our growth rate is still around two per cent per annum, which means that we are adding 20 million human beings to our nation every year, a figure equivalent to the entire population of Australia. It is quite obvious that such a heavy growth will strain to the utmost our efforts to provide the inputs that I have mentioned above, but I still detect an element of negativity amongst our planners regarding this issue. In fact I was shocked when a senior functionary to whom I mentioned population control immediately remarked that this term should never be used "because women's organizations object to it". I cannot understand the logic behind this. It is the women who bear the brunt of unplanned population growth both during and after pregnancy, and it is women's organizations which have to become much more active in this field so that rural women in particular are encouraged to adopt the small family norm. If this is not done, our aim of eliminating poverty is likely to be indefinitely postponed.

One of the dilemmas of our developmental process lies

in our inability to mobilise the active co-operation of the people. Decades ago when the Community Development Programme began under Pandit Jawaharlal Nehru, the idea was that the entire community would be involved in the process of development and that government would simply provide the necessary financial resources and administrative structures to promote this. Unfortunately, the reverse has happened. People everywhere now expect government to undertake even minor developmental works. The concept of *shrmadaan* has virtually disappeared, and there is a massive leakage of resources due to corruption at almost all levels as a reslut of which it is estimated that hardly 10 to 15 per cent of the funds sanctioned for rural development really get to the people for whom the programmes are designed.

The recent passage of the *Panchayati Raj* Act, perhaps Rajiv Gandhi's greatest achievement, might reverse this trend provided the *Panchayati Raj* institutions at all levels are genuinely committed to developmental projects and do not get involved in corrupt practices or caste conflicts. The one-third reservation for women in all *Panchayati Raj* institutions is indeed a progressive, even revolutionary step, and could in the long run bring about a grass-roots transformation especially in the rural areas. In fact the empowerment of women is a *sine qua non* for any substantial breakthrough in our battle against poverty.

This brings mc to thc final point I wish to makc in this chapter, and that is the exponential growth of corruption which like an acid is eating into the very heart of the nation and adversely affecting our economy, our society and our polity. It is a shame and a disgrace that a nation founded upon the noble principles of our freedom movement, with our national motto being *Satyameva Jayate*—Truth alone triumphs—should have got bogged down in a morass of corruption and nepotism. Our electoral system in itself is vitiated at the very start because of the huge sums of money that are required to secure a party ticket and to fight an election. Added to this is the growth of mafias and private armies in many parts of the country, often based upon caste and class considerations. The doctrines of implacable and inevitable class and caste warfare are, to my mind, a distortion of the basic principles that underlie not only our Constitution but our civilization. The ancient concept of working, thinking and achieving together without hatred represents far nobler ideals. This is not to say that outmoded feudal and economic structures should not be changed, but simply to point out once again that violent and corrupt means are seldom the best way to achieve desirable ends.

Breaking the poverty barrier will require a period of sustained effort by all sections of society, specially those who have in fact moved up the economic ladder and are now engaging an unprecedented degree of posterity. The extravagant and vulgar display of wealth at weddings and other social functions does not go well in a country where millions live on the verge of starvation. I am not advocating a grey austerity. In fact our festivals and ceremonies give life and colour to our whole social existence. And yet there should be some limits to ostentation. If those who can afford it were to put aside ten per cent of their budget for charitable purposes it could help to improve the quality of life of millions.

What is needed is the development of a social conscience, an awareness that howsoever prosperous we may be, we must not forget our debt to society. In our tradition we are all expected to repay four debts—*matri rin*—debt to the mother who nourishes us in her body and during our childhood, *pitri rin*—debt to the father who supports us until we can stand on our own; *guru rin*—debt to our teacher(s) who open for us the eye of knowledge, and finally *samaj rin*—our debt to society at large without which we would not flourish as a collective entity.

6

I believe that politics will always be turbulent because that is the nature of politics, as it is the nature of the sun to be hot and water to be wet, and that we must face boldly the battle of life into which we find ourselves precipitated. I believe that, approached in the right spirit, political activity can be a powerful instrument for human transformation and can thus contribute substantially to the broader goals that lie before the human race.

The word politics has of late assumed a very negative connotation, being generally perceived as involving corruption, defections, horse-trading and floor crossing, not to speak of the uproarious scenes that are witnessed in both Houses of Parliament and that are now telecast for the whole country to enjoy ! This is indeed unfortunate, because in a democratic polity, politics has a central role to play. Indeed without a healthy political and party system, the successful function of a democracy is simply not possible. We are justifiably proud of having established and maintained a vigorous democratic system ever since independence and the adoption of our unique Constitution almost six decades ago, and we are often held up as being a model for other post-colonial regimes, many of which are under either hereditary monarchies or military dictators. However, with all our democratic achievements, our political system has thrown up some clear weaknesses which need to be addressed.

The first is that the electoral system itself, although technologically very advanced with electronic voting machines which are not available even in the world's older democracies, is vitiated because of the huge sums of money that are expended in securing party tickets and then fighting the elections. The Election Commission has certainly introduced some useful reforms, but they have still not touched the heart of the problem. In a vast country like India with millions of people in each parliamentary constituency, fighting elections is necessarily an expensive undertaking. Of late the putting up of banners and other avoidable paraphernalia has been somewhat regulated by the Election Commission, but further steps need to be taken to reduce expenditure, including the possibility of the state funding to recognised political parties. This is a complex issue but it does need to be tackled otherwise money power will continue to distort the electoral process.

The second problem is our "first pass the post" system, whereby whoever wins a seat is usually supported by not more than 30 per cent of the electorate, and it is even possible to win with half that margin if there are a large number of parties and candidates contesting. In the result, hardly any Member of Parliament or the Legislature actually enjoys majority support in their constituency, and this necessarily leads to frustration and instability. A simple method has been suggested whereby after each election, if no candidate has received more than 50 per cent of the votes, on the very next day a second election is held between the two leading candidates. With electronic voting this is now quite a feasible proposition and it will ensure that whoever wins does enjoy the support of a majority of voters. This matter should be seriously considered by political parties, and a national consensus evolved as it will transform the whole political scenario in the country.

The third problem with our democracy is the growing nexus between criminals and politicians, highlighted several years ago in the Vohra Report. The growth of mafia and private armies often based upon caste and class considerations brings an element of tension and confusion into our democratic polity. Some measures need to be urgently taken to ensure that persons with proven criminal backgrounds are not able to contest for elections. After the last Lok Sabha elections, a leading journal published a shocking figure stating that there were criminal cases against more than one hundred Members of Parliament. Obviously one cannot disqualify a person simply on the basis of a charge, as that would lead to widespread misuse, but anyone who has been convicted should certainly not be able to contest. Simply making a statement regarding criminal cases is hardly the solution.

Then there is, of course, what has come to be known as Naxalite violence which is perpetuated by groups and parties that place themselves quite deliberately outside the pale of the constitutional structure. They are representing an increasingly serious threat, having extended their own activities in over a hundred districts covering several states all the way from the Nepal border down to Andhra Pradesh. This is essentially a law and order-cum-economic development problem which has to be tackled in all seriousness. If it is allowed to grow it will not only weaken our polity but ultimately even overthrow the constitutional structure which is their avowed intention, as expressed publicly through their websites. It is significant that much of the Naxalite activity is in the areas inhabited by our tribal communities, towards whose welfare special attention needs to be paid.

The fourth point is with regard to federalism. Our Constitution, the largest in the world, has set out in detail the federal structure of the nation, but has also included provisions for central intervention through Governor's rule. Clearly this was envisaged as a last resort in the event of a breakdown of law and order or an unbridgeable constitutional deadlock. Unfortunately, however, over the years it has often become a mechanism for the ruling party in the Centre to dismiss governments not to their liking. The Sarkaria Commission has made some valuable recommendations not only in this respect but with regard to entire function of the federal system. These need to be implemented without delay, as a dilution of federalism is having a detrimental impact on our democracy in the long run.

Some years ago I chaired a group called the IIC-Constitution Committee which spent a year studying in depth the functioning of the Constitution and making certain concrete recommendations for its better working. Unfortunately neither the report of this Committee, which was a civil society initiative, nor the report of the Constitution Review Committee headed by Chief Justice Venkatachalaiah have been seriously considered for implementation. As I have said, shorn of its weaknesses, political activity has a crucial role to play in the whole exercise of development and poverty alleviation. It is important that the negative perceptions regarding politics and politicians that have now become widespread, largely through the Bollywood movies which inevitably portray politicians as venal and corrupt, should be rectified. While it is too much to expect that politicians will become paragons of virtue, it is surely possible to bring back at least a minimal degree of probity and prestige to the political system.

Another factor which is beginning to impact our political structure is the consolidation of regional parties and the relative decline of all-India parties, specifically the Congress and the B.J.P. The Congress under Sonia Gandhi made a dramatic comeback in the 2004 General Elections, but we still have only 145 seats in a Lok Sabha of 547. While coalitions are well accepted, multiple small parties together cannot really provide the political gravitas needed for a coherent and consistent political and economic policy. Dependence on support from the ruling combine also injects an element of instability and unpredictability into the whole political structure.

We seem gradually to be moving towards a three-front model: a Centre-Left Front led by the Congress; a Centre-Right Front led by the B.J.P. and a Left Front led by the CPI (M), which are in fact the three largest parties in the present Lok Sabha. If it consolidates, this three-front pattern can bring a certain stability and consistency into our political system. The need for dedicated and committed politicians, however, will remain an essential prerequisite for national development and cohesion regardless of the changing electoral equations. We are proud of our democratic system, but quite clearly the time has come for substantial in-flight corrections, and the sooner these are made the better it will be for the nation.

7

I believe that our generation holds the present in trust for posterity, and that we have to fulfil this responsibility so that we can repay the debt we ourselves owe to the past. I believe that we must, therefore, protect this planet from wanton despoliation and blatant exploitation in the name of progress, that we must conserve its atmosphere and water, its forests and wild life, from the destruction they are facing as the result of increasing urbanization and industrialization.

It has been well said that we have not merely inherited our natural environment from our ancestors, we have in fact borrowed it from future generations. One of the most disturbing features of the 20th century has been the attrition that has taken place as a result of human intervention in the natural environment. Millions of acres of forest land have disappeared, thousands of species of flora and fauna have become extinct, the life-giving rivers that have nourished the human race have become highly polluted, the air that we breathe is contaminated and even the land beneath our feet has been poisoned by an unbridled use of pesticides and chemicals. Global warming has been rising apace, resulting in what is known as the greenhouse effect whereby temperatures are rising around the planet, and the ozone layer which protects us from harmful solar radiation is steadily attenuating. Glaciers around the world, including the Himalayas, are receding at an alarming rate and the whole process of pollution has gathered an accelerating momentum.

Several attempts have been made to mobilize world opinion in this regard. I was a member of the Indian delegation, led by the then Prime Minister, Shrimati Indira Gandhi, to the first Conference on Human Environment held in Stockholm in 1972 which resulted, among other things, in setting up the United Nations Environment Programme (UNEP) with its headquarters in Nairobi, Kenya. This was followed by the Conference in Rio, Brazil, twenty years later in 1992, and the signing of the Kyoto Protocol in Japan in 1995. However, the norms set down for the reduction of carbon by the affluent Western nations have been ignored particularly by the United States of America, which consumes more energy per capita than the rest of the world put together. Some countries in Europe, such as the Scandinavian ones, do indeed have an excellent record in this regard, but overall the picture is grim and forbidding. The increasing growth and developmental activity in the two huge Asian countries of China and India will necessarily result in an increase in carbon emission. The world is facing one of its most serious crises in the form of environmental destruction and global warming, and along with terrorism they represent the greatest challenges to humanity in the 21st century. Unless they are overcome they will result in chaos, conflict and destruction.

Our ancient literature exudes a profound awareness of environmental values. The whole concept of sacred groves and rivers, springs and forests was designed to emphasise the fact that human beings were not divinely endowed with the freedom to exploit and destroy nature at will, but rather are a part of the natural environment which it is their duty to protect. The *Bhoomi Suktam*, Hymn to the Earth of the *Atharva Veda* (XII.I) in its 63 verses has a remarkably comprehensive statement of environmental values. To quote just one verse:

> "Whatever I dig from thee, O Earth,
> May that have quick growth again.
> O purifier, may we not injure thy vitals or thy heart"

As far as wildlife is concerned, having been closely associated with this for several decades I feel a special sense of sorrow at the manner in which it is disappearing. It is interesting to recall that when Indira Gandhi asked me to become Chairman of the Indian Board for Wildlife soon after I joined her Cabinet in 1967, I discovered to my surprise that since independence our national animal had been the lion evidently because of the Ashoka-lions on our national crest. However, lions were found only in one corner of the country in the Gir forests in Gujarat, whereas the magnificent tiger was spread throughout the country from Uttaranchal in the North down to Karnataka in the South, and from Rajasthan in the West to Assam and West Bengal in the East. I therefore persuaded the Board to pass a resolution that the national animal should be changed from the lion to the tiger and this was approved by the Prime Minister and the Cabinet.

Simultaneously we launched the Project Tiger with a Steering Committee under my chairmanship, and we chose nine tiger reserves in various States to begin the process of intensive conservation of this magnificent animal. It needs to be stressed that the tiger, although beautiful in itself, is only a symbol of the zoological pyramid in each reserve, so that Project Tiger would help in preserving the entire flora and fauna of the reserved area. The project, which was wholly funded by the Government of India, was supported by the WWF, the World Wildlife Fund now known as the World-Wide Fund for Nature, and the State Governments also were co-operative.

At that time we had estimated that against around a hundred thousand tigers at the turn of the century, hardly 3000 or so had survived the hunting instincts of the British Viceroys and the Indian princes, and the criminal activities of the organised groups of poachers. For the first ten years during which I remained Chairman of the Steering Committee, Project Tiger was considered to be perhaps the most successful conservation project in the world. Unfortunately after the Congress defeat in the 1977 elections, the political will behind this project rapidly evaporated, and we have now come to a position where prime sanctuaries such as Sariska in Rajasthan have lost every single tiger, and reports from other sanctuaries are also deeply disturbing.

It could be asked that when people are starving why should we concentrate upon tigers. The answer is, of course, that while the process of poverty eradication must be speeded up, the natural environment also has to be preserved for generations yet unborn. If all our forests were to disappear it would wreak havoc in the sense that trees are basically producers of rain water and only secondarily for wood. Without them the weather pattern would change disastrously, soil erosion would assume menacing proportions and all the beauty of our forests and the well-being of those who live near the forests would be in jeopardy.

While on the question of forests, it has been my experience that corrupt practices have wrought havoc at least in the Himalayan region. I once said in Parliament that where there is an unholy trinity consisting of a corrupt politician, a corrupt contractor and a corrupt forest officer, whole forests can disappear and resurface in the form of posh colonies that are developing around the country. This is not to say that all politicians, contractors and forest officers are corrupt, but if such people do get together they can do terrible damage as has indeed occurred in the sub-Himalayan ranges.

It is also, of course, essential to provide alternative sources of fuel for cooking and heating purposes to the rural population so that the necessity to cut down forests is reduced to a minimum. Tribal and other communities living in or near forest area should continue to enjoy the advantage of collecting firewood and other minor forest products. However, to parcel forests out to individual families is to invite decimation within a decade. Forests have always been looked upon as community and state property, and so they must remain if they are to continue to exist at all. As it is, satellite pictures show that our forests cover has already shrunk to much less than the official figure.

There are many other aspects of the problem of conservation including the Himalayas which, having for centuries been our protector, now demand protection from us. Environmental safeguards need to be adopted in the planning process as far as major projects are concerned, but more importantly the *Panchayati Raj* institutions must be encouraged to take up afforestation (reforestation) programmes at the rural level. Also, environmental values must become a significant part of our educational programmes so that young people grow up with a sense of awareness regarding the importance of preserving and improving our natural environment.

The whole question of the environment is one that by definition cuts across national barriers. The protection and preservation of the Himalayan environment, for example, will involve six countries—Pakistan, India, China (Tibet), Nepal, Bhutan and Bangladesh. So also global warming and the rising of the ocean levels will not respect any man-made divisions, and there is a real apprehension that within the next few decades several island nations may in fact disappear from the face of the earth. Our concerns for the environment, therefore, must necessarily be global, although we have obviously to concentrate upon what we can do in our own country. In this context an excellent document is the Earth Charter which was drawn up after prolonged and widespread consultations with experts from around the globe, and finally released by the Earth Charter Commission in March 2000. It combines environmental and Interfaith principles in an effective and practical manner, and should become the basic document for the global society along with the Universal Declaration of Human Rights.

8

I believe that life is necessarily a mosaic of joy and sorrow, of pleasure and pain, of failure and success, of shadow and sunlight; that we must accept these dualities as a necessary stage in our spiritual progress until we are able to transcend them; and that each experience can be a valuable means for inner growth, unpleasant situations often affording greater opportunities for development than superficially pleasant ones.

Life, in my view, is not merely what Bertrand Russell called "a fortuitous conglomeration of atoms", but a unique opportunity for spiritual growth, a lifelong learning experience. The journey from the womb to the tomb, or the pyre, is one in which each individual encounters a vast variety of experiences, both pleasant and unpleasant, and each one of these, if addressed with a positive mindset, can represent a valuable learning experience. We all wish for pleasant happenings throughout our lives, but often have to face the opposite. Apart from the continuing onslaught of poverty which makes life a burden for many, those from the affluent sections of society have often to face physical and emotional traumas.

In my own life, it so happened that by the age of eighteen I had spent as many as eighteen months in bed, mostly flat on my back. This was as a result of a hip condition that refused to disappear and for which I was sent to America for treatment. After over a year in hospital in India and America, and a major operation, I had literally to re-learn how to walk, first with two crutches, then with two canes, then with one cane. Within six months of my return from America I was involved in a motor car accident in which I broke my leg and injured the hip again. This time I was bedridden for six months and had again to undergo a major operation.

Looking back, although the events were extremely painful and agonizing, I feel that the year I spent in the United States for the whole of 1948, when affairs in my home State were in turmoil, enabled me to develop a broader perspective on national and international events, to undertake some intensive reading, brush up my chess and start watching television which had only just been introduced. In other words, even that prolonged stay in hospital became a learning experience and helped me for the rest of my life to deal positively even with negative events. I have recorded these events in some detail in my autobiography (Oxford University Press).

In politics also there is necessarily the same mixture of triumph and tragedy. I recall winning elections comfortably from the Udhampur constituency four times—in 1967, 1971, 1977, and 1980. Even in the post-Emergency election of 1977, when Indira Gandhi and each one of her other Cabinet ministers from Northern India was defeated, I won my election with a comfortable margin. However, in 1984, after the dastardly assassination of Indiraji by her own bodyguards, I made the miscalculation of changing my constituency from Udhampur to Jammu, where I stood as an Independent. I had evidently overestimated my political strength in what was my 'home' constituency and, in the event, lost decisively. This was clearly a traumatic event for me, used as I was to winning all previous elections, and it would be dishonest for me to claim that I was not deeply hurt. However, again looking back now, I find that perhaps it was a blessing in disguise because it enabled me to break out of the rut of elective politics for a full ten years, during which period I travelled around the world, deepened my involvement in the Interfaith and environmental movements and developed a persona independent of political affiliations.

It so happened, of course, that I again got involved in elective politics when I was chosen for the Rajya Sabha in 1996, though I resigned that seat in 1998 and was re-elected in 2000. In 1999 I was asked to take on the formidable task of challenging the sitting Prime Minister and three-time M.P. from Lucknow, Atal Behari Vajpayee, then the most powerful political figure in India. With a notice of less than a fortnight before the election was to begin, my wife and I launched a vigorous campaign in a constituency that was entirely new to me. I was able to poll a respectable number of votes and to slash the Prime Minister's margin by a hundred thousand. Also we tied him down to Lucknow for the last four days of the campaign. This time I did not feel any negative emotions for having lost, but in fact was rather pleased that we were able to take on a Herculean task and put up a creditable performance. I may add that in all these six parliamentary elections that I have fought, my wife has been an invaluable asset and has helped tremendously, particularly to bring out the women voters.

One of the secrets on my spiritual path is to try and develop the capacity to maintain an inner core of detachment regardless of how thick the battle outside rages. If one can stand back, as it were, and watch oneself as if from outside, the whole situation takes on a different dimension. To my mind this is one of the key teachings of the 'Gita', which says that the battle must be fought but with a sense of detachment and without any obsession regarding the result. Some people may feel that such an attitude would lead to lukewarm activity, but in fact the reverse is true. The sense of inner detachment gives us a deeper perspective into the whole situation and prevents us from getting overwhelmed by the tremendous upsurge of physical and emotional activity that is inevitably involved in such events.

Joy and sorrow, in fact, represent the warp and woof of the fabric of life, and are as inevitable as night and day. It is this duality that needs to be transcended if we are really to reach our spiritual goal, and clearly this can only be done if we find within ourselves a spirtiual centre that is unaffected by outer changes. That spiritual centre in turn has to be linked with whatever form of divinity we may choose to worship. I am a worshipper of Lord Shiva and try to follow the teaching—*yat yat karma karomi tad tad-akhilam Shambho tavârâdhanam*—whatever action I perform I look upon as an offering to Shiva. This is a talisman that helps to carry us through the adventure of living, whether the object of our devotion is Shiva or Krishna, the Goddess or Jesus Christ, or any other.

In my "Essays on Hinduism" I have tried to encapsulate

the message of the *Upanishads* and the 'Bhagawadgita' which represent the high watermark of Hindu thought. I am sometimes asked as to what is my position regarding those who do not believe strongly in any particular religion. The answer is that if each person acts from what they consider to be their highest ideal, provided it does not involve violence or coercion of any other human being, all will be well. At their highest, all religions teach the religion of humanism, of love and harmony. In this context there is a "Hadith" from the life of the Prophet Mohammad. Once when he was in Medina a funeral procession passed by and he stood up in respect for the deceased. His followers exclaimed that the dead man was not a Muslim but a Jew. The prophet is said to have replied, "But was he not a human being?"

9

I believe that love and friendship constitute the surest bonds in a world where everything is constantly changing, and that these should be cherished whenever and wherever they are found. I believe that the creation of beauty through music and poetry, the fine arts and architecture, is a central function of civilization and must be encouraged so that increasingly large sections of society can derive the intangible but extremely valuable benefits that flow therefrom, so that we can be led from the outer beauty of form to the inner beauty of spirit. I believe, further, that our system of education should be designed to inculcate in the young an awareness of the primacy of the spirit, without in any way belittling the importance of the material foundations upon which any dynamic civilization must rest.

The emotional and aesthetic dimensions of human existence have generally received little importance, obsessed as we are with political and economic developments. In fact it is these subtle but in some ways even the more significant elements in our inner lives that can either help to create a fully renewed and integrated personality or, if neglected and distorted, wreak havoc with our personalities.

To begin with the emotions, human beings are creatures endowed not only with a brain but with feelings, and over the millennia these have developed into two broad categories. One is the instinct to fight, to hunt, to kill, to dominate, and this involves not only animals but fellow human beings also. The whole of human history is full of unspeakable horror and cruelty perpetrated by man upon man, whether it was the ancient conquerors Changiz Khan, Alexander, Taimur or in more recent times the horrors of Hitler's gas chambers and the Gulag archipelago, Guantanamo or Abu Ghraib. These negative instincts, including the master element of fear, continue to reside in the psyche of human beings around the world, and it is these that have brought about all the horrors and indignities that the human race has inflicted upon itself down through the long and tortuous corridors of time.

Fortunately, there is a countervailing set of emotions which include love, friendship, compassion, mercy and forgiveness. These also have always existed since human civilization began, but have often been overwhelmed by the more aggressive and negative emotions. If we are to move into any kind of inner integration and outer harmony, it is essential that we transcend the negative emotions as they can literally kill not only other people but ourselves. Hate, anger and jealousy can be every bit as lethal as cancer, AIDs and heart disease. These psycho-somatic linkages are now being increasingly recognized by medical practitioners around the world, while for those on the spiritual path they form the bedrock of their praxis.

Love and friendship particularly are the master keys which bring positive elements into our consciousness. Love has many forms. Arjuna mentions only three when he demands from Krishna the love of a father to his son, of a friend to a dear comrade and of a true lover to his beloved. The sovereign vibration of love knows no boundaries of caste or creed, religion or nationality, sex or sexual preference. Indeed it is strange that in India we still carry on in our statute books absurd Victorian norms regarding various forms of sexual activity, which not only criminalize a considerable section of our population but also represent a major impediment in the anti-HIV/AIDs programme that is so vital for our national welfare. The world over now it has been recognized that sex or sexual activity between consenting adults, men or women, is something that should be left to their good sense. Of course, any use of force or exploitation of children for sexual gratification are totally unacceptable and need to be severely punished. However, we need to liberalize our laws as has been done in almost all the progressive modern democracies around the world.

True friendship again is something that has an indefinable quality which cuts across conventional barriers of social status. Therefore, as I have said, in a world that is constantly and rapidly changing—that is the Sanskrit definition for the world, *Sansâra,* that which is constantly changing—these should be cherished whenever and wherever they are found. The friendship between Krishna and Sudama, Castor and Pollu, Sri Rama and Hanuman, all represent different facets of the master emotion—Love. Again a very deep relationship exists between teacher and disciple, *guru* and *shishya* in all civilizations. Socrates and Plato, Shams Tabriz and Jalaluddin Rumi, Pir Nizamuddin and Amir Khusro, Sri Ramakrishna and Swami Vivekananda provide glowing examples of the manner in which human and divine love can coalesce into a symbiotic unity.

Along with these positive emotions, an important dimension of human consciousness concerns the creation of beauty through many forms—music and painting, literature and poetry, fine arts and architecture, dance and dramatics. Whether or not this has any quantifiable values in terms of the GDP, the fact remains that the creation of beauty has been one of the major driving forces in human civilization.

The beautiful cathedrals of Europe, the amazing rock cut caves and carvings of Ajanta and Ellora, the glorious Taj Mahal, the astounding Angkor Vat complex in Cambodia, all represent efforts to combine religious aspirations with the creation of beautiful structures. Modern Japanese architecture, the great paintings and other art objects in museums around the world which I have had the privilege of visiting, such as the Hermitage in Leningard, the Albert and Victoria in London, the Prado in Spain, the Metropolitan in New York and numerous others, are redolent with beauty. While this may be considered an unaffordable luxury for those still battling at the subsistence level, for those who are above it the nurturing of positive emotions and the capacity to respond to beauty is a significant element and these should be included in our educational curricula.

From the spiritual point of view, the journey is from the outer beauty of form to the inner beauty of spirit. In the final analysis it is true that beauty lies in the eyes of the beholder, because it is from the spiritual depth of the beholder that the capacity to access and appreciate beauty arises. What is more beautiful than looking up at the heavens during a moonless night and seeing millions of celestial bodies shining in all their glory? It is an awesome sight, particularly in the higher elevations, and reminds us that these stars were in existence long before our solar system came into being and will continue for millennia.

In comparison with them our lives may be but a moment in the continuous flow of time, but the glory is that we are endowed with the capacity to comprehend our condition and to respond creatively to the beauty around us. Indeed there is a view that our consciousness is in fact a function of an evolving universe, and that we are not mere atoms floating on the broad ocean of time but live in a participatory universe, so that by our inner growth we can contribute to the unfolding of the cosmic destiny. This would indeed be the crowning miracle of human existence.

A special word here needs to be said about music, that universal language which is one of the glories of human civilization. Music has played an invaluable role in my own life, and I have had the privilege of participating in three very different streams of the musical tradition. The first was *Dogra-Pahari* folk music which I heard on my mother's lap and which became an integral part of my life ever after. Recently I have recorded two CDs of *Dogri bhajans* and *Dogra-Pahari* folksongs for HMV. The second is the Hindustani classical music tradition. My father was a connoisseur, and got me started on *riyâz* from the age of ten. I still practice regularly once a week, and as a boy recorded several *ragas* for HMV meant for private circulation.

The third element may surprise some readers. I have been an ardent rock/pop music fan ever since Bill Hailey and the Comets began the rock revolution way back in the early fifties. Since then I listen regularly to pop music, my favourites down the years being Cliff Richard, Harry Bellefonte, the Pet Shop Boys, Abba, Billy Joel, Dire Straits and Whitney Houston. I also enjoy the Strauss waltzes, and the Blue Danube, of course, is a perennial favourite.

Music is of course a powerful instrument for spiritual growth. *Bhajans* and the glorious Sanskrit *stotras* mellifluously recited are of incalculable value in sharpening the mind and cleansing the heart. *Natanam Âdinar* brings Shiva *Nataraja* to life in a way that no other medium can, while hymns to Krishna, Rama, *Karthikeya* and the Goddess are also full of spiritual vibrations. The chanting of the *Vedas,* the Gregorian chants in the Christian tradition, the expert recitation of the 'Quran', the singing of the 'Guru Granth Sahib' which is set entirely to *ragas* and *talas*, melody rhythm, are all proof of the central role that music can play in the spiritual quest.

10

I believe that while each one of us owes a deep debt to the country of our origin, as members of the human race we also owe a wider loyalty to the planet that has nurtured our kind for millions of years.

The whole question of multiple identities has become a necessity in the emerging global scenario. The old concept of 'one person one identity' is no longer valid, because it restricts our consciousness to a unidimensional level. Let me give my own example. I have a *Dogra* identity based upon the ethnolinguistic community known as *Dogras* who played such a significant role in extending and consolidating the northern frontiers of India in the 19th century by founding the composite State of Jammu & Kashmir. The *Dogri* language, our folk songs, *pahari* paintings and other traditions form an important part of my consciousness and my *Dogra* identity.

I have a regional identity in that I belong to Jammu & Kashmir, the State founded by my intrepid ancestor Maharaja Gulab Singh. I have a caste identity, which is still virtually inevitable in Hindu society. As a *Rajput* I was brought up on the tales of *Kshatriya* valour and chivalry going all the way back to my namesake *Karna* in the

Mahabharata and coming down to Maharana Pratap. Chhatrapati Shivaji and others. This also, combined with Rajasthani folk songs, palaces and forts, remains a significant part of my consciousness, and represents a *Kshatriya* identity.

Then, I have a Hindu identity. All my life I have been reading the Hindu classics, particularly the *Upanishads,* which to my mind are the high watermark not only of India but of the world's philosophy, as well as numerous luminous commentaries such as Sri Aurobindo's "Essays on the Gita" and Sri Krishnaprem's "Yoga of the Kathopanishad". Hindu myths, symbols, traditions, temples and pilgrimage places represent a significant factor in my consciousness and indeed I have written and spoken extensively around the world on *Vedanta.*

Then there is my identity as an Indian. I am proud to be the citizen of a nation that has played such a long and distinguished role in the development of world civilization, that has given birth to four of the great world religions and welcomed many others to her fold, the country described in the shastras as *Âa setu Himalaya paryanta*—from Rameshwaram all the way up to the mighty Himalayas, a nation that has adopted a Constitution that has enabled us to work a vibrant, democratic polity with a free press, independent judiciary and fundamental rights that are justiciable and enforceable, free of chaotic elections, and the rule of law.

I have lived all my life in India, although by a curious concatenation of circumstances, which I have recounted in my autobiography, I was born in the beautiful Mediterranean town Cannes in France. I landed in India with my parents when I was six weeks old and have lived here ever since except for a brief sojourn of seven months as Ambassador to the United States and, of course, I have travelled literally all the five continents of the world. I have been involved in Indian politics at the regional and national level, have represented it in numerous official and non-official functions around the world. Also, having met Mahatma Gandhi, having been influenced by Jawaharlal Nehru whom I consider to have been my political *guru*, and having worked as a Cabinet colleague with Indira Gandhi for a decade, I have participated in decision-making process at the highest level. I have also been a member of the *Lok Sabha* for eighteen years and in the *Rajya Sabha* now for ten years. Hence my Indian identity is extremely significant.

However, there is a yet larger identity to which I belong, and that is as a resident of Planet Earth, a global citizen. However much each one of us may cherish the country of our origin, we must begin to realize that as members of the human race we also owe a wider loyalty to Planet Earth that has nurtured our race for billions of years up from the slime of the primeval ocean. Indeed the most beautiful photograph ever taken is the one of Planet Earth taken from outer space. That shows our planet as it really is, a tiny speck of life and light against the unending vastnesses of outer space, so beautiful and yet so fragile. I have always felt that this photograph should hang in every classroom in every country around the world, so that children grow up with the realization that with all their patriotism they have a broader commitment to Planet Earth, and that it is the environment of this planet that all of us have collectively to preserve and protect.

I must add that as long as one looks upon these multiple identities as emerging from a spiritual centre, or as concentric circles, their number can increase ad infinitum without creating any problem. It is only if the centre begins to change with each identity that one becomes eccentric and distorted. I find that my identities are not only mutually supportive, but also open my consciousness to other parallel identities. Thus as a *Dogra* I have close relationship with the Kashmiris with whom we have been associated since the mid-19th century and the Punjab from where our family rose to prominence. I also seem to have some special Tamil *Samskaras,* as I am fascinated with the *Nataraja,* with the 63 *Shaiva* saints known as the *Nayanmars* and with *Bharatanatyam.* As a *Kshatriya* I interact with all communities, particularly those who have been so shabbily treated in history. As a Hindu from a Muslim majority State, I am active in the Interfaith movement which involves a continuing interaction with members of all the great religions of the world. As an Indian I have friends around the world and have always tried to further regional and global harmony.

Thus there is a vertical dimension to identity beginning with the ethno-linguistic and moving on to the global, as well as a horizontal dimension in which each identity interacts creatively with parallel identities in each particular dimension. The rapid spread of globalisation in our own lifetimes has now made it imperative for each one of us to broaden our consciousness and extend the circumference of our identity. The very subsistence of human life on this planet over the next few centuries may well depend upon whether or not we can shake off the narrow confines of sectional, denominational and fundamentalist thinking and open ourselves to the winds of change that are sweeping across the planet *Upanishads* say—*âa no bhadrâh kritavo yantu vishwatah* "Let noble thoughts come to us from every side."

11

I believe that death is a natural and necessary corollary to life, and must be accepted in a positive manner rather than with fear and dread. I believe that the death of the body merely marks another step in the long journey of the pilgrim soul towards its final destination, and that man must shake off the superstitious dread that he has with regard to this essential and inescapable phenomenon. One of Lord Shiva's appellations is Mahakaleshwar, the Great Lord of Death, and when He is ready, so am I.

In the same way as day and night, joy and sorrow, shadow and sunlight are linked in an unbroken cycle, life and death also constitute a cyclical process. I do not believe in the concept of one single life. In fact all the four Indic religions—Hinduism, Jainism, Buddhism and Sikhism—believe in rebirth, and this gives one a different perspective of life than if we believe only in a single lifetime. Indeed, considering the tremendous variety of experiences that are needed to grow towards spiritual enlightenment, having a single life would seem to be like going to school for only one day and being expected to learn the entire curriculum.

Theology apart, the concept of rebirth is linked closely with the theory of *karma* whereby we are the makers of our own destiny. Far from being a fatalistic philosophy, *karma* is a great declaration of independence because it holds that by our actions we can make or unmake our future in this and subsequent lives. Whereas in the West they talk of 'life and death', in the East it is 'birth and death', 'Life' transcends both, and the concept is that through various paths we can at last directly access the divine and break the cycle of births and deaths in which all beings are inexorably caught up.

Each religion has a theory as well as a methodology of transcendence. In Hinduism, as I have pointed out, there are four great paths to enlightenment—*Jnâna yoga*, the way of wisdom; *Bhakti yoga*, the way of devotion; *Karma yoga,* the way of dedicated action; and *Râja yoga*, the way of psycho-spiritual praxis. Each one of these or a combination thereof, if pursued with sufficient diligence and continuity has the power, to enable us finally to break the cycle and attain a stage of consciousness which does not necessitate rebirth. Whether thereafter consciousness merges permanently into the divine, thus attaining *moksha* or *nirvana*, or whether by a deliberate act such realized beings can continue to exist at some level to help the struggling humanity, as in the case of the *Siddhas* and the *Bodhisattvas*, is then a matter of free choice. It is believed that through *yoga* one can attain an immortal body, as the *Shwetâshwatar Upanishad* says—*na tasya rogo, na jarâ, na mrityuh, prâptasya yogagnimayam shariram*—there is neither illness, nor old age, nor death for one who has obtained a body made of the fire of *yoga*.

In some societies death is not supposed to be mentioned and, as it were, is put behind us. In the Hindu tradition, however, *Yama,* the god of death, is right out in front and worshipped along with other deities on special occasions. There are also fascinating stories in our literature regarding human beings having conquered death, notably the story of *Savitri* and *Satyavan* in the *Mahabharata,* upon which Sri Aurobindo has based his splendid poem *Savitri,* and story of the great Shiva devotee *Markandeya,* and of *Nachiketa* in the *Kathopanishad.* In other religious taditions also there are descriptions of angels, archangels, *Bodhisattvas, Arihantas* and other such beings who are outside the widespread net of death.

Finally I might mention what is still a controversial issue and that is of voluntary death. I am not speaking here of euthanasia, which involves assisting in the death of people either in intolerable pain or in a vegetative state. I go much further, and feel that if we seek to control birth why should death remain disorganized, unexpected and chaotic. Why should it not be possible for people who feel that they have completed their task in this lifetime, to be able to go peacefully and painlessly through a judicious mixture of lethal and psychotropic drugs. Indeed several decades ago, when I was Health Minister, I wrote an article entitled "In quest of the Nirvana Pill", which I reproduce below :

> "I am glad that Shobori Ganguli in her article, 'Death: positive solution for life negative' (January 13, 1999), has dealt with a matter which I have been raising now for a quarter of a century. The right to die in peacc and dignity, at a time and place of one's choosing, has still, unfortunately, not been universally accepted as a fundamental human right. While in the West there has been a movement in this direction, as is evident from books like "Last Rites" by Marya Mannes and "Final Exit" by Derek

Humphrey, as well as the play, "Whose Life is it Anyway ?" the acceptance is still very limited and revolves mainly around the question of euthanasia. As has been pointed out by Ms. Ganguli, this flows from a basic belief of certain religions that we have only one life on earth, and therefore it must be preserved at all costs even though it may have become a living hell.

"As against this, the Indic religions—Hinduism, Jainism, Buddhism and Sikhism—believe in a constant series of rebirths until one achieves spiritual illumination. It follows, therefore, that death is looked upon as a necessary counterpart to birth. As the "Gita" says in Chapter 2, verse 27, "One who is born has inevitably to die, and one who has died has inevitably to take birth again, therefore, for what is inevitable, you should not grieve." The Indic religions speak not of life and death, but of birth and death, both being transcended by the greater Life.

"In these religions it is well known that spiritually advanced individuals often choose the time and place of their departure from this world. The "Gita" (Chapter VIII, verses 12 & 13) clearly states the prcedure whereby an enlightened person can voluntarily drop his body, and both in Jainism and Buddhism there are techniques in which the body can be deliberately starved and discarded. The point, therefore, is well taken that we should develop our own approach to this vexed problem of voluntary death. Mr H.D. Shourie's book, "Voluntary Exit" is a welcome effort in this direction.

"As Health Minister a quarter of a century ago I had privately mooted with some top scientists the possibility of exploring what, for want of a better term, I called a Nirvana pill, which would combine lethal and hallucinogenic substances to enable a person to leave the world painlessly and joyously whenever he or she deems it fit to do so. We do not have to wait until we are racked with unbearable pain before taking such a step.

"Indeed it would be ideal if, when persons feel that they have fulfilled their obligations and are ready to drop the body, they are enabled to do so at a time, place and atmosphere of their own choosing. With startling developments in the fields of chemistry and pharmacology, the preparation of such a pill should not be difficult. We have no compunction in regulating birth, but death still remains disorganized, unplanned and usually messy and traumatic. Would the earth not be a happier place if a painless and dignified exit could be ensured?

"I am well aware that such a procedure is not possible within the present legal structure, where suicide is looked upon as a criminal act, the only crime in which if you are successful you cannot be punished, but if you fail you can be incarcerated!

> This whole matter calles for a widespread public debate among intellectuals, social workers, organizations of the elderly, medical professionals and concerned citizens. Possibilities of misuse, indirect pressure and intimidation, of course, are there and must be minimized. But surely it is time that we look at the whole question afresh, especially as the elderly population around the world is steadily growing and, along with it, the number of people who are seeking a swift and peaceful voluntary exit."

Whether or not one accepts this theory, I feel that death itself can be a powerful learning experience, and that instead of facing it with fear and horror, we should be able to address it in a calm and positive attitude. Apart from removing the constant "fear of death" that hangs over the minds of most people, such an attitude would also expedite whatever transition lies beyond the death state.

12

I believe, finally, that a divine destiny pervades the cosmos, a destiny not distant and remote but one in which, in some mysterious way, each one of us is actively involved. I believe that the most effective means of fulfilling that destiny is a combination of active outer involvement in furthering human welfare and intense inner striving to reach the goal of spiritual realization. I believe, thus, that the most eloquent prayer that has ever been evolved is one that has resounded in India down through the corridors of time since the very dawn of our civilization:

From illusion lead me unto Reality,
From darkness lead me unto Light,
From death lead me unto Immortality.

The whole question of whether there is any sense or purpose behind the cosmos, or whether it is entirely an evolutionary development from the original Big Bang, is one that has engaged the attention of philosophers and scientists for thousands of years. Originally, with the geocentric model, we tended to give exclusive importance to Planet Earth as if it were the centre of the universe. With the Copernican revolution, it became clear that we were a minor planet circling around the sun, thus developing a helio-centric model. With recent developments in cosmology, satellite technology and the astounding photographs of the cosmos that these have produced, it now transpires that there are billions of stars like our sun in our own Milky Way galaxy, and millions of galaxies in the observable universe. On that cosmic scale our planet bears the same relationship to the cosmos that does a single grain of sand to planet earth.

With such immensities of space comes also the awareness of vast aeons of time that have elapsed since the universe began. Some suggest 12 billion years, and it is therefore perhaps presumptuous for human beings to assume that they have any cosmic sginificance. And yet there are persuasive theories that hold the opposite view. George Wald, the Nobel Laureate, postulates a mind-breeding universe in which the evolution of consciousness is in fact the goal of creation, even though it may have taken billions of years to achieve. Evolutionary philosophers such as Sri Aurobindo in the East and Teillard de Chardin in the West have postulated the evolution of human consciousness to higher and higher levels as being the final goal of evolution. Pir Vilayat Khan speaks of a participatory universe in which each one of us is in fact an active factor in the unfolding of the divine plan. There are many other fascinating theories including Rupert Sheldrake's theory of cosmogenetic resonance, Stanislav Grof's extended cartography of the brain, as well as cosmological beliefs built into various religions.

As against this, Arthur Koestler holds that human beings are a species programmed for self-destruction because of an engineering defect in the human cortex whereby the thinking and the feeling functions are inadequately integrated. As a result, although we know the disastrous consequences of certain actions, such as, for example, the development of increasingly powerful weapons of mass destruction and supportive systems, we continue with this path because our emotions are stronger than our intellect. As *Duryodhana* says in the *Mahabharata:*

"I know what is *Dharma,* but I am not attracted to it,
I know what is *Adharma,* but I am attracted to it."

Are we simply a fortuitous conglomeration of atoms or, as Professor Vilayamir Ramachandran would have it, of neurons? Are we simply meaningless specks of complex matter buffeted hither and thither by fate and *karma,* or do human beings have a positive role to play in the evolving universe? These are tantalizing questions to which there are no clear-cut or definitive answers. However, as a hypothesis, the idea of human consciousness being able to co-operate with the evolutionary thrust gives it a sense of direction as it confronts what would otherwise be a meaningless existence. Thus each human life is one that is imbued with significance, both for the individual and the human race.

In my view, we have to make some such assumption if our lives are to have any meaning beyond simply our own existence. The idea that a divinity pervades the entire cosmos, what is manifest and what is yet to be manifest, is central to the *Vedanta—Ishâvâsyamidam sarvam yatkimcha jagatyâm jagat*—as the *Upanishad* says. If we further postulate the existence of a spark of that divinity within ourselves, then our spiritual striving acquires a deep significance, which is why I have postulated in my twelfth belief that the most effective means of fulfilling our destiny is a combination of active outer involvement in furthering human welfare and intense inner striving to reach the goal of spiritual realization.

The vision of the cosmic dance of Shiva, where millions

of galaxies spring into being every moment and millions are extinguished in the unending cycle of eternity, is only now beginning to reflect the knowledge that we are receiving from our initial probings into the universe around us. And yet, within all these vastnesses, perhaps because of them, remains the eternal mystery of the human personality. Among billions of galaxies one is ours; among billions of stars in this galaxy one is ours; among billions of living beings in this solar system one of them is ourselves, but such is the grandeur and mystery of the human personality that it can move towards a comprehension of the unutterable mystery of existence. We who are children of the past and the future, of the earth and the heavens, of the light and the darkness, of the human and divine, at once evanescent and eternal, of the world and beyond it, within time and in eternity, yet have the capacity to comprehend our condition, to rise above our terrestrial limitations and, finally, to approach the incredible possibility of transcending the throbbing abyss of space and time itself. That is both the mystery and challenge of being human.

Glossary of Sanskrit words and their meanings

âa setu Himalaya paryanta, 92 — from Rameshwaram in South India all the way up to the Himalayas

adharma, 109 — unrighteousness

anantakoti brahmanda, 28 — infinite millions of galaxies

arihantas, 101 — Jain religious prophets

Atharva Veda, 69 — one of the four Vedas, the holy scriptures of Hinduism

atman, 17 — the soul

bhajans, 88 — devotional songs

bhaktas, 19 — devotees

bhakti yoga, 18-19, 100 — the spiritual path of devotion

bharatanatyam, 94 — India's most ancient and famous classical dance form

bhoomi suktam, 68 — hymn to the Earth in the Atharva Veda

bodhichitta, 17 — Buddha's nature

bodhisattvas, 101 — highly evolved beings who stay back in the earth consciousness to help suffering humankind *chakras,* 21 — seven psychic centres within the human body, from the base of the spine up to the brain

dharma, 109 — righteousness; law of right behaviour

Dogra, 91, 94 — an ethnic group residing in the Jammu region and Himachal Pradesh known for their valour

Dogra-Pahari, 87 — miniature paintings done by artists in the Dogra region

Dogri, 91 — mother tongue of the Dogras, included in the Indian Constitution

Dogri bhajans, 87 — devotional songs in Dogri

Duryodhana, 108 — a major negative character in Mahabharata

Ekatvam, 18 — oneness; unity with the divine

Guru, 85, 93 — spiritual teacher; greatly revered in the Eastern tradition

Guru rin, 55 — debt to the spiritual teacher

jnana yoga, 18, 100 — the spiritual path of intellectual discrimination

karma, 99, 109 — actions

karma yoga, 18, 20-21, 100 — actions as well as the theory, that our past and present actions influence our future spiritual status

Karna, 91 — the tragic hero of the Mahabharata

Karthikeya, 88 — the second son of Lord Shiva mounted on a peacock, widely worshipped in South India

Kshatriya, 91, 92 — the warrior in the old structure of the caste system

Kathopanishad, 101 one of the most important and impressive of the Upanishads which, collectively represent the high watermark of Hindu philosophy

kundalini, 21 a spiritual force believed to reside at the seat of the spine. With certain yogic practices it can be aroused to travel up the 7 chakras, ultimately flooding the brain with spiritual light and power

Lok Sabha, 93 the lower house of the Indian Parliament

Mahabharata, 92, 101, 108 one of the two great Hindu epics, the other being the Ramayana

Mahakaleshwar, 11 one of the names of Lord Shiva, Lord of death/time

Markandeya, 101 a youth deeply devoted to Lord Shiva who rescued him from the jaws of death

matri rin, 55 debt to the mother—There are considered to be three debts when one takes birth—to the mother, to the father and to the teacher (spiritual guru)

moksha, 100 liberation from the cycle of birth and death

Nachiketa, 101 the boy who questions Yama, the God of death in the Kathopanishad

natanam âdinar, 88 the famous dance of Shiva; title of a Tamil devotional song

Nataraja, 88, 94 the dancing Shiva; statues are now known around the world

nayanmars, 94 — 63 Shaiva saints from Tamilnadu who lived over a thousand years ago. Their lives are recorded in the Periya Puranam

nirvana, 100 — a Buddhist term relating to higher spiritual achievement

pahari, 91 — from the hills

Panchayati Raj, 53, 72 — elected local body institutions in India

Panchsheel, 45 — the five foundations of Buddhist philosophy

pitri rin, 55 — debt to the father

ragas, 87, 88 — melodic structures in classical Indian music

raja yoga, 18, 21, 100 — the spiritual path of Gnostic practice including breathing, physical postures and awakening of Kundalini

Rajput, 91 — same as Kshatriya (the warrior, which existed in the old structure of the caste system)

Rajya Sabha, 93 — upper house of the Indian Parliament

rishi, 43 — the illumined Hindu sages who composed the Vedic hymns

riyâz, 87 — regular practice of any art, particularly music

samaj rin, 55 — debt to society

samskaras, 94 — impressions from past lives and actions

sansâra, 85 — the world around us which is constantly changing

satyameva jayate, 54	truth alone triumphs, the national motto of the Indian State taken from the Mundakopanishad
Satyavan-Savitri, 101	a husband and wife whose story is to be found in Mahabharata. Savitri's devotion brought her husband back from death
Savitri, 101	Sri Aurobindo's great poem is also called 'Savitri'
shaiva, 94	related to Shiva
shishya, 85	disciple
shrmadaan, 53	a voluntary contribution through physical work
Shwetâshwater Upanishad, 100	one of the best known Upanishads
siddhas and the Bodhisattvas, 100	great beings who, having attained the possibility of moksha/nirvana, decided to stay back in the world in order to help those who are struggling for enlightenment
Sindhu, 42	an important river in North India, also a word for the ocean
stotras, 88	Sanskrit devotional hymns dedicated to various deities
Sufis, 19	Muslim mystics, most famous of whom was Maulana Jalaluddin Rumi
talas, 88	metrical system in Indian music
tirthankara, 42	24 Jain prophets of whom the last was Lord Mahavira

Upanishad(s), 7, 17-18, 28, 79, 92, 95, 109	title of inspired spiritual texts in Sanskrit representing the high watermark of the Indian philosophical tradition
Vedanta, 7, 92, 109	another term to collectively describe the Upanishads
Vedas, 41, 88	the holiest scriptures of Hinduism, four in number—Rigveda, Yajurveda, Samaveda and Atharwaveda
Yama, 100	the God of death in the Indian mythological tradition
yoga, 17-19, 21, 46	literally to join. The philosophy of unity of Atman with the Brahma, or of God immanent with God transcendent

मुद्रक : लक्ष्मी प्रिंटइंडिया, शाहदरा, दिल्ली-32